CONTENTS

CHAPTER 1

GAME On!

Brandi Coffman puts on her headset. She switches on her video camera and takes a deep breath. Her teammates' voices fill her headphones. They talk about how to win. The game begins.

BRIGHT IDEA BOOKS

THE Truth ABOUT LIFE AS A Pro Gamer

by Ciara O'Neal

Raintree is an imprint of Capstone Global Library Limited, a company incorporated in England and Wales having its registered office at 264 Banbury Road, Oxford, OX2 7DY – Registered company number: 6695582

www.raintree.co.uk
myorders@raintree.co.uk

Edited by Charly Haley
Designed by Laura Graphenteen
Original illustrations © Capstone Global Library Limited 2021
Production by Melissa Martin
Originated by Capstone Global Library Ltd
Printed and bound in India

978 1 4747 9559 3 (hardback)
978 1 4747 9723 8 (paperback)

British Library Cataloguing in Publication Data
A full catalogue record for this book is available from the British Library.

Acknowledgements
We would like to thank the following for permission to reproduce photographs: iStockphoto: adamkaz, 12–13, 23, Cecilie_Arcurs, 20–21, damircudic, 16–17, ohishiistk, cover, 29, RyanKing999, 8–9, 28, stray_cat, 11; Shutterstock Images: Dean Drobot, 26–27, Gorodenkoff, 5, 14–15, Maridav, 25, nazarovsergey, 19, Ohishiapply, 6–7, Sergey Novikov, 30–31
Design Elements: Shutterstock Images

Coffman is a professional video gamer. She has played games like this many times. But she still feels excited. Her heart races.

Pro gamers work together on a team.

Light flashes across the screen.
Coffman ducks her character
behind a wall. She looks around.
A teammate is in trouble. She
makes her character run to help.

Minutes later, she cheers.
Her team wins the match! This
puts her team in first place
in the **tournament**. They win
prize money.

There are tournaments for
many different video games.

Tournaments are one way Coffman
makes money. Tournaments can have big
prizes. Some pay thousands of pounds.
Other prizes are much smaller.

Gamers can use webcams to make videos of themselves.

Gamers can use webcams to make videos of themselves.

After the tournament is over, Coffman wants to share her win with others. She replays a video of her match. She records herself talking about it. She talks about the good things she did. She shows her mistakes. Then she puts the video on YouTube.

Videos are another way Coffman makes money. Gamers can get paid for **streaming** on websites such as Twitch or YouTube.

TWO WAYS TO PLAY

Pro gaming is often called Esports. Tournaments can be played online or in person.

CHAPTER 2

BECOMING A
Pro Gamer

Gamers who want to be pros work hard. First they pick a game they love. Then they practise a lot. Many families already have computers or gaming **consoles**. This is all that is needed to start playing.

Being a pro gamer can start with playing video games at home.

TEAMS AND LEAGUES

Pro gamers don't just play against their friends. They compete against other pros. They join teams and **leagues**. These groups help them learn better ways to play. They also give gamers the chance to play in tournaments. As players improve they can join better leagues.

Pro gamers compete in big tournaments.

LEAGUES

There are many leagues gamers can join. One example is Major League Gaming. Another is the Overwatch League.

PRACTISING AND LEARNING

Most pros train for six to eight hours a day. They practise clicking fast. They play a level again and again. All this practice helps them to get better.

Pro gamers must study too. Coffman searches the internet for new ways to win. She watches videos of other pros playing. She wants to learn how to improve.

Pro gamers are serious about practising. Teammates practise together.

Gamers study their games to learn new skills.

GAMERS AROUND THE WORLD

Anyone can work to become a pro gamer. Gamers can be any age. They live all over the world. They can speak any language.

Each video game has its own rules. Players learn different skills with each game. Good players spend hours learning more about their game. Some even employ coaches to help.

CHAPTER 3

THE GOOD AND
the Bad

There are many good things about being a pro gamer. Most gamers love playing. They spend a lot of time doing what they love. They can win money too.

But pro gaming is not easy. Sometimes pro gamers feel like they need to win. They may feel **stress**. This can make gaming less fun.

Gamers can feel unhappy when they lose.

Pro gamers work hard. Video games change and become harder. Pros must keep learning to stay at the top of their game.

Gamers may get tired if they play too much. They may even feel sick.

Gamers must also be careful. It can be unhealthy to play too much. There is a disease called gaming disorder. Doctors say this happens when gamers cannot stop playing.

CHAPTER 4

LIKE EVERYONE Else

In many ways pro gamers are just like everyone else. They want to have fun. They work to become good at what they do. They need to take care of themselves.

Pro gaming teammates cheer when they win.

It is important for pro gamers to exercise and eat healthy foods. Gamers spend a lot of time sitting in front of computers. Looking at a screen all day can hurt their eyes. Gamers need to be active while not gaming. Many teams have a daily exercise routine.

Sometimes pro gamers struggle like everyone else. Even a great player might not make enough money. They may need another job.

Like all people, pro gamers need to eat healthy foods.

Some people who love gaming decide to make games.

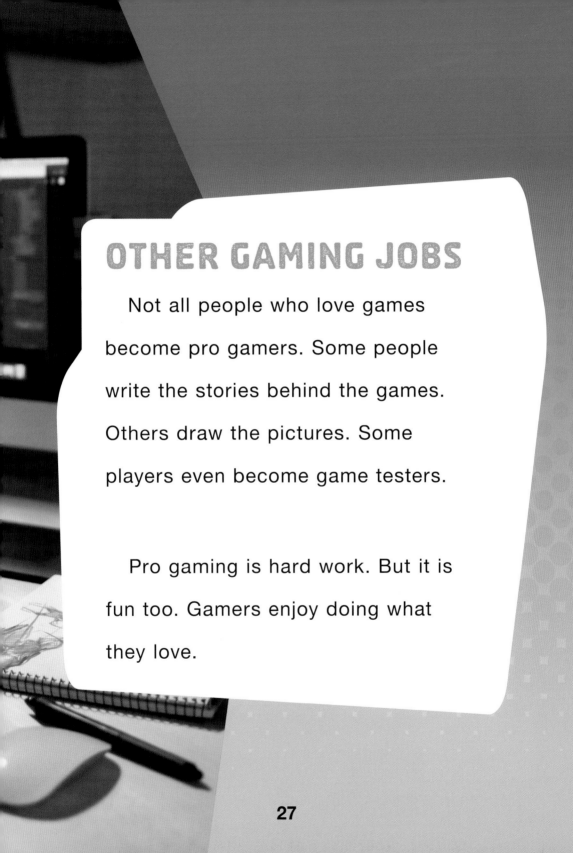

OTHER GAMING JOBS

Not all people who love games become pro gamers. Some people write the stories behind the games. Others draw the pictures. Some players even become game testers.

Pro gaming is hard work. But it is fun too. Gamers enjoy doing what they love.

GLOSSARY

console
type of computer used to play video games

league
group of teams that compete against each other

streaming
showing videos online, often with comments

stress
worry or bad feelings about needing to do something or about something in the future

tournament
competition that involves teams playing several matches of one game

TRIVIA

1. **Victor De Leon III** of the United States is one of the youngest pro gamers. He started playing when he was 2 years old.

2. In 2012, **Kathleen Connell** from the UK was one of the oldest gamers. She was 100 years old.

3. Pro gamer **Kuro Takhasomi** of Germany earned more than £2 million in 2019.

ACTIVITY

HOST A GAMING TOURNAMENT

Pro gamers compete in tournaments. There are several matches in a tournament. The team that wins the most matches wins the tournament.

You can host a gaming tournament with your friends or family members. Choose your favourite two-player video game or computer game. If you do not own one, see if you can borrow one from your school, a library or a friend. Get everyone to take turns playing against each other in a tournament. Watch and cheer for each other as you play. When someone loses a game, they are out of the tournament. Winners keep playing until there are only two people left. The winner of that last match wins the tournament!

FIND OUT MORE

Books

Awesome Video Game Competitions (Cool Competitions), Lori Polydoros (Raintree, 2017)

Computer Games Designer (The Coolest Jobs on the Planet), Mark Featherstone (Raintree, 2013)

Ralph Baer: The Man Behind Video Games, Nancy Dickmann (Raintree, 2020)

Website

www.bbc.co.uk/newsround/31767504
Can playing video games help you with your homework?
Find out more about this interesting study.

INDEX